new father's
survival guide

new father's
survival guide

MARTYN COX

RYLAND
PETERS
& SMALL
LONDON NEW YORK

Senior designer Toni Kay
Commissioning editor Annabel Morgan
Picture researcher Emily Westlake
Production Toby Marshall
Art director Leslie Harrington
Publishing director Alison Starling

First published in the UK in 2010
by Ryland Peters & Small
20–21 Jockey's Fields
London WC1R 4BW

First published in the United States in 2010
by Ryland Peters & Small
519 Broadway, Fifth Floor
New York, NY 10012

www.rylandpeters.com

10 9 8 7 6 5 4 3 2 1

ISBN 978-1-84597-955-3

A CIP record for this book is available
from the British Library.

Printed and bound in China

Neither the author nor the publisher can
be held responsible for any claim arising
from the use or misuse of suggestions
made in this book. While every effort has
been made to ensure that the information
contained in the book is accurate and
up to date, it is advisory only and should
not be used as an alternative to seeking
specialist medical advice. Consult your
doctor if you are concerned about any
health issue affecting your child.

contents

introduction 6

plans and preparations 8
baby comes home 38
important practicalities 80

picture credits 112

introduction

Whether you've been a singleton for years or living together as part of a couple, becoming a dad for the first time is an exciting but often daunting prospect. Up to this point you've only ever really had to think about yourself, but from now on you'll have a family to consider, and you'll face new challenges every day as your child grows and develops.

It may be a much-used cliché, but it's also entirely accurate when you hear parents say that having a baby completely changes your life. The second you set eyes on your new baby, you will feel an enormous urge to protect them, while the responsibility of nurturing and providing for a child gives you a sense of maturity that makes your former life without baby seem somewhat trivial.

To ensure that the transition from life as a couple to living as a family is as seamless as possible (although it's unlikely that this switch will be entirely without hiccups), there are plenty of things to get to grips with before your new baby arrives on the scene. So how do you deal with the arrival of a tiny person who is about to completely change your life? Well, in the words of the Boy Scouts, you need to Be Prepared.

As a father of two, I muddled my way through my partner's first pregnancy, which resulted in a boy, but felt like a complete expert by the time she gave birth to our daughter. Of course, every birthing experience is different, but my first-hand knowledge, along with advice from many of my male friends who have become new parents, should be helpful to any father-to-be.

This little book isn't a replacement for those in-depth scholarly guides or medical reference books. I'm not an expert in child psychology or parenting, but an ordinary dad who hopes to offer some down-to-earth, practical tips that may make becoming a father easier.

Along with advice on how to prepare yourself in the run-up to the birth, what to do when the big day rolls around and what to expect when baby comes home, there's practical information on choosing a buggy/stroller, kitting out your car and baby-proofing the house.

Congratulations on becoming a new father. It's going to be a bumpy – but thoroughly enjoyable – ride!

plans and preparations

thinking ahead

Well done – you're going to be a dad! Sounds good, doesn't it... but maybe slightly scary at the same time, as you come to terms with the fact that you're leaving the life that you know and are comfortable with for unfamiliar territory!

Although you might have a while to wait until the big day, time will fly past, and before you know it, you'll be gazing into the eyes of your baby. Some men do absolutely nothing to prepare for fatherhood, choosing to coast along until their partner gives birth, but failure to do any groundwork is guaranteed to result in a rude awakening when baby arrives!

The months running up to your partner's due date can be fun and rewarding. Use them to spend time together, to discuss the future and talk over any anxieties you might have. It's a time to plan and make preparations. Consider where to give birth, enjoy decorating the nursery and start to amass all the kit you'll need. It also gives you the chance to buy a new pair of wheels... sorry, I mean a buggy/stroller!

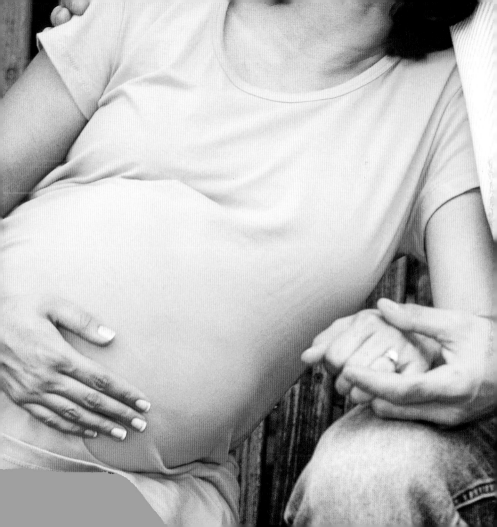

important choices

Deciding where to give birth is generally a decision you will make together, but as your wife or partner is the one who has to do all the hard work of bringing the baby into the world, it is more diplomatic (and probably fairer) to allow her to have a bigger say. Generally, the choice is either to give birth at home or in hospital. Some couples will prefer a home birth, as they feel more comfortable in their own surroundings, but this does require a lot of forward planning and you may need to hire specialist equipment, such as a birthing pool.

By far the most popular place to give birth is in hospital. Your GP/obstetrician may recommend a hospital, or you might like to visit a couple of different hospitals before you make up your mind which one you prefer. Looking round is a bit like going on a

tour of a historic building, with plenty of expensive equipment that you're not allowed to touch and a guide (generally a nurse or midwife) who knows their subject matter inside out. After showing you around the facilities, you'll get the chance to ask questions, and by the end of the visit you'll have a fairly good idea about whether you would like your partner to give birth in that hospital or not. Don't let first impressions put you off – a midwife at one hospital we visited (who had an uncanny resemblance to a prison guard I had seen on a TV show) announced that she 'didn't take any nonsense from fathers', which didn't endear either her or the hospital to me. Yet the very same midwife assisted at the birth of my son, and she turned out to be very helpful and a lovely person whose bark was definitely worse than her bite.

Those with doubts about a hospital should garner the opinions of friends or neighbours with kids. If the response is negative, you can consider different options. However, bear in mind that it's not a good idea to choose hospitals that are far away, as you will visit a few times during the course of the pregnancy for ultrasound scans/sonograms and may well need to get there in a hurry for the birth.

ultrasound scans/sonograms

Well before you get to hold your baby, you'll have the opportunity to see it developing inside your partner, thanks to ultrasound scanning/sonography. At least two scans are generally carried out during pregnancy. The first takes place between 8 and 12 weeks, when measurements are taken, and a second scan usually takes place between 18 and 22 weeks, when the sonographer takes a more detailed look at your baby.

Due to work commitments, I missed the opportunity to be present at the scans/sonograms of my first child and had to make do with a grainy picture of the foetus, which, quite frankly, could have been a picture of absolutely anything – although I still managed to convince myself that I could see him smiling! However, I did make it to the scan/sonogram of my second child, and seeing her tiny limbs moving on the screen was an emotional moment. For the first time, that lump inside your partner's belly becomes a real baby… don't worry, you can cry at this point if you want to!

At the second scan, the sonographer may be able to tell you the gender of your child. Do you find out the sex or not? We chose not to, but some soon-to-be parents want to know for practical reasons. If you don't want to know, mention it beforehand, otherwise the sonographer may inadvertently let the cat out of the bag.

well read

Check out the bookshop shelves and you'll find a glut of guides covering every single aspect of pregnancy, childbirth and bringing up baby. It's inevitable that one or even a huge pile of them will find their way into your home and the question every expectant father has to ask himself is: 'Should I read them?' Well, I can honestly say that I didn't read anything, leaving that to my partner, who read her way through what seemed like an entire library of books. Why didn't I read them? Not because I was being selfish, neglecting my duties or would rather watch paint dry, but rather because everything my partner read was faithfully relayed to me, proving that the ancient form of passing information by word of mouth still works.

More seriously, reading a general guide on pregnancy and childbirth is a good idea, as it will show you are taking an active interest in the weeks before, during and after birth, and will also ensure that you know exactly what your partner is going through. It will also help you to understand all the technical jargon that you will hear when you visit the doctor or hospital. And following the birth of your child, you will find that a good book on childhood illnesses is an essential tome to have close at hand.

back to school

If you thought your education came to an end the day you graduated from college, then think again. Like any other subject you have no experience of, parenting is easier if you have a little bit of training to prepare for the whirlwind that's about to hit your life. Although you may choose to do absolutely nothing and simply rely on your instincts to get you through the early weeks of new parenthood, you will undoubtedly feel perplexed, worried or in need of help at some stage. Accordingly, it's wise to enrol for parenting classes so that you have some idea of what to expect.

Actually, parenting classes are nothing like school. They're informal, the groups are small and you don't need to raise your hand if you need to go to the toilet. Oh, and you won't leave with a qualification at the end either. Held in hospitals, town halls, schools and libraries, the classes usually take place on a weekly basis and last for a couple of hours.

Parenting classes broadly cover what to expect during the birth and when baby comes home, offering expectant parents good advice, information and the chance to learn new skills, among them some breathing and relaxation techniques that will help your partner with the birth. Another benefit is the opportunity to meet other dads-to-be living in your area and to make new friends.

If, for whatever reason, you are unable to attend a course of parenting classes, or you decide that you don't want to go, you'll find that there are a multitude of online forums, chatrooms and blogs that you can visit to glean advice on the birth and dealing with a newborn. If you have a specific question, you can leave a message and wait for a response from other readers.

When your baby arrives, you may want to investigate early-days classes, which offer support and help with the reality of new parenthood, whether you're in need of tips on how to soothe a crying baby or on dealing with sleep deprivation.

You might not believe it possible at the moment, especially if you have been together for many years, but once you are a family it becomes difficult to remember what it was like when it was just the two of you. Despite family life feeling incredibly natural (for many of us anyway), it's worth making the most of your last days as a couple. After you've bought all the gear, decorated the nursery and made plans for the birth, there's nothing better than spending some time together before the big day. If it's close to the due date, choose a long weekend, but while the expectant mother is able to fly (most airlines allow pregnant women to fly up until 28 weeks), you could go further afield. A recent phenomenon is the babymoon (think honeymoon for those about to have a baby) and canny travel agents have put together packages specifically for couples about to become a family.

Apart from spending time together as a couple, make sure you catch up with friends or colleagues in the evenings. Once the baby is on the scene, it will be difficult to continue in the way you did before. Your help will be needed at home, especially in the early days, and even if your partner gives you a 'pass' to go out for the night, you'll probably find you want to rush home to spend time with your new little family!

couple time

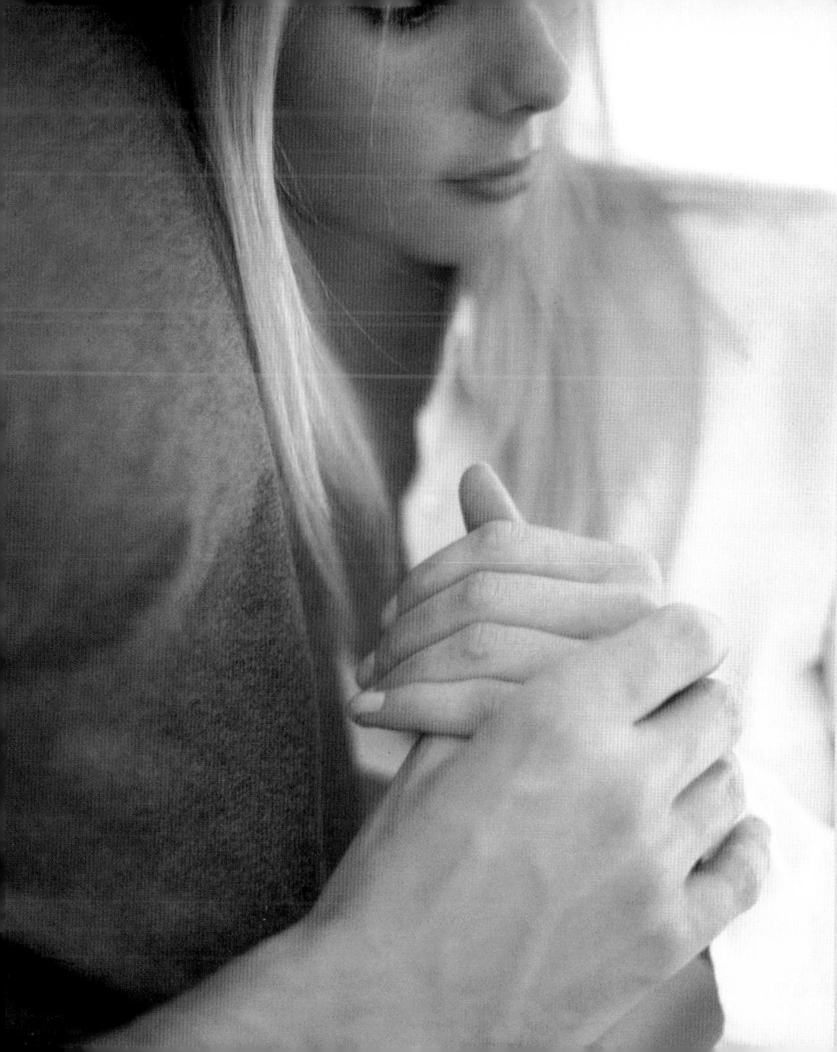

birth survival kit

Expectant mothers are instructed to pack a bag of essential items to take to hospital with them, including clothes, items for the new arrival and toiletries. It's a good idea for the dad-to-be to put together his own birth survival kit. The time to do this is a few weeks before your partner's due date, which will avoid you having to race around in a frenzy at the last minute when she announces that she has to go to hospital NOW – the chances are that under such pressure you are likely to forget something.

First of all, money is essential. Most hospital car parks have parking fees, so ensure that you have plenty of loose change to pay for parking during the stay. Plenty of change is also useful for purchasing snacks and drinks from vending machines, which may be your only option for subsistence if you arrive at hospital in the middle of the night when cafés, snack bars and hospital shops are all closed.

A mobile phone will be needed to keep your friends and family informed of progress. Make sure you have all the important numbers stored on your phone so that you can avoid insulting important family members such as your partner's parents – if they are the last to discover that they have just become grandparents, you'll be in their bad books for life.

Unless you have lots of spare time after the birth (which is very unlikely), you might want to set up a phone tree, which makes letting lots of people know about the safe arrival of the baby very simple. To do this, you will need to call two people (both sets of parents, perhaps), who will then call two more people each, who will then do the same and so on. This may require a little bit of time to set up in advance, but is fairly foolproof and should ensure that nobody is forgotten about and thus offended!

A camera or camcorder is essential to capture the first precious moments with your new child, while a magazine or book is useful if there's a lull. It goes without saying that you shouldn't even think about putting your feet up with your chosen reading matter and a cup of coffee during labour. It would be so wrong! Although you might not get time for a shower at the hospital, it does pay to have a few toiletries with you so that you can freshen up – all you need is a toothbrush, toothpaste and a deodorant.

If you have the time, try and make some sandwiches or have some food and drinks that you can grab from the refrigerator before heading for the hospital. During your partner's stay, she will be catered for by the hospital, but you will have to fend for yourself. If it's a long labour and she needs you around to reassure her and keep her calm, you might not get the chance to pop out and grab a snack in the hospital. Having something to keep you going will ensure that you don't start to flag.

offering support during birth

During the actual birth, there may be moments when you feel like a useless bystander, but have no fear, your presence will be noticed and gratefully received by the mother-to-be. It goes without saying that all the hard work during labour is undertaken by your partner, yet you still have a fundamental role to play in offering her both physical and emotional support.

You can bring her glasses of water, sponge her head if she is hot and give her shoulder, feet or hand massages to help distract her from labour pain. During the very last stages of labour (known as transition), you can help her to concentrate on pushing and breathing, and hold her hand to give her plenty of reassurance (be prepared to stifle the occasional yell of pain when she crushes your hand tightly during contractions). During the birth of my first child, I even had to deputize for a stirrup to support my wife's left leg, as the one from the delivery room had gone missing. The chances of this happening to anyone else must be slim, but do expect the unexpected…

If you've opted for a hospital birth, you'll be in a slightly intimidating and alien environment, and your familiar face will provide security and help her to concentrate. Even though you may feel a little bewildered by the whole experience, don't remain silent. Encourage your partner and be reassuring, telling her how well she is doing.

To ensure that you are prepared for the whole birth experience, you'd better enrol on those parenting classes now, or the event might completely take you by surprise!

eureka! meeting your baby for the very first time

Most of us have had a moment in our lives where we have experienced an overwhelming sense of emotion and excitement. For me it was passing my driving test as a teenager after the sixth attempt – I felt completely elated to have got my licence after what felt like years of trying. However, nothing, not even that moment, compares to the exhilarating moment that you first set eyes on your new baby.

After nine long months of waiting, buying clothes and equipment, of planning and watching your partner's bump growing, touching her belly and feeling the baby respond, and helping her through labour, the instant you first see your child is the single most exciting, emotional, invigorating and humbling thing that will ever happen to you – I promise.

For me, there was also a palpable sense of relief. Pregnancies do not always run smoothly and our son became distressed while his mother was in labour, leading to the obstetrician swiftly arranging for an emergency Caesarean to take place. I held her hand as a team of surgeons

operated and sat numb, absolutely glued to my seat, as a midwife received the tiny body and hurried him over to a resuscitation team. There was no sound from him and his body was floppy. I was terrified that something was wrong and squeezed my partner's hand in fear, then spontaneously burst into tears when I heard his first tiny cry.

The moments that follow are some of the best you will ever experience. Mine were spent holding and gazing at my son, a precious, tiny little bundle wrapped up in a blanket, while my partner was being stitched up and moved to a bed in a recovery room nearby. She was given our baby and then the pair of them lay together with me on a chair next to them. It was our first time together as a family and a calm, relaxing moment compared to the frightening experience we'd been through.

if things don't go
according to plan…

After baby has arrived, you'll all want to get home as soon as possible to start your new life together as a family. If everything goes smoothly, you can expect your partner to be discharged from hospital between 24 and 48 hours of giving birth – maybe even sooner if there are no problems and she had a straightforward delivery.

However, if there were complications, or if your baby was born via an emergency Caesarean section, then you must be patient, as your partner will need to stay in hospital a while longer, until her doctors are satisfied that she is making a good recovery.

Generally, a woman who has given birth by Caesarean section will stay in hospital for three to four nights, or even longer if she (or her doctor) feels that she needs more time to rest and recover. As an emergency Caesarean will have taken you both completely by surprise and was not part of the birth plan, you will have had no time to consider what to do in the event of such circumstances.

During this time you are likely to be using either paternity/family leave or your holiday/vacation entitlement, and it's important that you visit your partner and baby on a daily basis, allowing yourself time to bond with your child, while giving your partner all the support and companionship you can.

Although you might want to remain at the hospital from the moment it opens to the time visitors are asked to leave in the evening, you might like to consider visiting in two daily shifts. Go for a few hours in the morning, then head home and do some household chores before returning mid-afternoon. It's important that your partner doesn't return home to a chaotic environment with lots of laundry and cleaning up to do. She will be exhausted and more than occupied with your beautiful new baby.

baby comes home

a new chapter

This is what you've been looking forward to – the moment baby comes home. It's an exciting, exhilarating time when you get to be a family for the first time. However, this new chapter in your life will also present you with new and unexpected challenges. Don't worry, there's nothing you can't handle. The keys to getting through the exciting weeks ahead are to talk to your partner, to expect the unexpected and to enjoy the new-found responsibility that comes with being a dad.

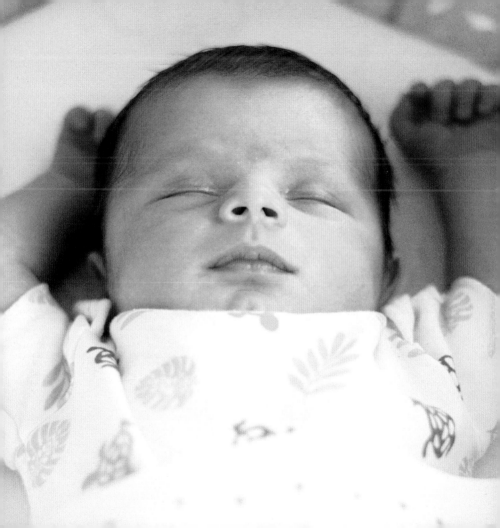

holding your baby

Many first-time fathers are intimidated about holding their baby at first – they look so terrifyingly small and fragile. Like everything else, it's a skill that's soon mastered with practice – you will quickly get used to handling them and will get over feeling slightly awkward, or worrying that you are holding them the wrong way.

There are many ways to hold a baby, but one of the easiest is to hold it close to your body, supporting baby's head and neck in the crook of one arm, while placing the other under its bottom. This is a great position, as you can look into each other's eyes.

Newborns are keen to be held, and love skin contact. This gives you the opportunity to take off your shirt and recreate the iconic 1980s sepia-hued poster 'Man and Baby', which sold 5 million copies worldwide and showed a muscular young man tenderly cradling a tiny infant. Not been working out recently? Don't worry, baby won't care what kind of physical shape you're in!

making the most of the early days

When your partner gives birth, you may be entitled to take some time off from work to get to know the new arrival. Paternity/family leave entitlements vary widely from country to country, and the duration can also depend on employers. Some will give you longer than the norm, or allow you to boost your leave by adding on some of your annual holiday/vacation entitlement (be careful not to take all your time off at the beginning of your new family life and leave yourself with very little later on). If you are self-employed, you'll know how much time you can afford to take off without working.

Paternity or family leave is a great opportunity for you to get to know your new baby better, and those men who use the time wisely will immerse themselves in helping to

care for their child – getting to grips with bathing, taking him or her for a spin in the buggy/stroller, changing, cuddling and putting baby down to sleep. Unless your baby is bottle fed, the obvious biological differences between male and female bodies prevent men from feeding, but you can always help wind him or her, or walk the floor during those inexplicable newborn crying fits or when baby refuses to settle.

While you're at home, you'll earn a great deal of love and appreciation from your partner if you roll up your sleeves and get stuck in to the domestic duties. Wash the dishes, make the beds, load the washing machine and tidy up. This is especially important if your partner has had a Caesarean section, as it counts as a major operation and she will not be back up to her normal speed for several weeks. You will also have to act as doorman. As soon as your partner is home, there is sure to be a flurry of requests from friends, family, colleagues and neighbours all clamouring to pay a visit, so you may need to restrict entry to ensure that it doesn't get all too overwhelming for mother and baby.

These early days pass all too quickly. However, if you've made the most of your time together, you'll have a firm bond with your new baby and some wonderful memories (and photos!) that will last you a lifetime.

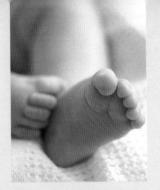

going back to work

Going back to work can be a wrench. Not only will you miss spending time with your baby, but it's more than likely that you will be preoccupied with thoughts of your partner and child, and how they're coping without you, so it can take a while to settle back into the normal routine. The first day back is the worst. Everyone will want to congratulate you, bombard you with questions, tell their baby stories or demand to see your photographs, so make sure you take plenty with you.

After this, it will be time to get on with work. Except you can't. You're either too tired and find yourself simply staring in a glazed fashion at the computer screen, or you can't get your baby out of your mind and want to call your partner every five minutes to see how she's getting on. There's no easy solution – you're going to have to muddle through as best you can and reward yourself by giving them a call at lunch time. It's easier said than done, but try and put mother and baby to the back of your mind and compile a list of jobs for the day, then work your way through them. The first day back to work is the hardest – it will get easier as you slot back into routine. If you find that after several months you're still desperate to be at home, you could investigate whether you could afford to work part-time or possibly change your hours by asking your employer about a flexible working pattern.

sleep deprivation

If you work in an office, you'll instantly recognize a new parent – they are the ones that arrive slightly late, have bloodshot eyes, look a little dishevelled and give a huge yawn the moment they settle down at their desk to start a day's work. Unfortunately, sleep deprivation comes with the territory when you have a baby. You're completely at your baby's mercy when it's hungry, as it will announce it wants food with an ear-piercing wail that will only cease when it gets what it needs. Usually, at the beginning, you'll be woken every hour or two through the night, depending on baby's routine (or lack of one!).

Although you may be able to snore off back to sleep between feeds, you might find you're still trying to drop off when it starts wailing again. I've never been a particularly deep sleeper and find it incredibly difficult to fall back to sleep when I've been woken. As a result, when my children were babies I spent entire days, weeks and months in what felt like a constant blur of tiredness.

Being exhausted is just about manageable when you're on paternity/family leave or during the weekend, but the sensation, which feels like a hangover or leaves you extremely spaced out, is not ideal when you're at work. A few weeks after the birth of my first child I was at a meeting at work that lasted about two hours. At the end I realized that I hadn't uttered a single word and couldn't recall anything that had been said. Fortunately for me, most other people in the meeting had children, so had been through the same experience themselves. If you have a sympathetic boss, it might be worth explaining to them that you won't be firing on all cylinders, although it goes without saying that not all managers have such warm hearts!

According to experts, adults need between seven and nine hours' sleep a night, yet most new parents are thought to lose an astonishing 350 hours of sleep over their baby's first year. Lack of sleep prevents the brain from functioning properly, causes your attention levels to drop and means that your ability to solve problems will be impaired. It can also make you just that little bit moodier than normal.

So what's the solution? Well, some men want to share the experience and support their partner, but realistically the occasional night in another room doesn't hurt and will ensure that you are not completely incompetent at work (and at home). If baby is bottle fed, you and your partner might want to take it in turns to do the 'night shift', which at least guarantees a nice, long undisturbed sleep every other night.

While you're right in the middle of it, this period may feel like it's going on forever, but fortunately the period of extreme sleep deprivation won't last – from about three months old, some babies start to sleep all the way through the night, or at least for longer periods of five to six hours in a row. Before you know it, you'll start to feel brighter, sharper and – at last – useful rather than useless at work.

dealing with your mother-in-law

You may have a wonderful relationship with your mother-in-law – in which case, congratulations. Or you may find that every time you meet, barbed comments are exchanged and you could cut the atmosphere with a knife. Most men probably fall somewhere in between. And no matter how much you enjoy your mother-in-law's company in small doses, the likelihood is that

you don't feel the need to spend too much quality time with her.

Unfortunately for those that have a prickly relationship with their mother-in-law, the birth of a daughter's baby is generally seen by both mother and daughter as an ideal time for your mother-in-law to come and stay. And although you may not be quite so thrilled by the idea, it's your partner's wishes that count at this time and she will probably be delighted to have her own mum there to help her muddle through the early stages of motherhood. Not only will they enjoy sharing these early days but your partner will hopefully pick up some parenting tips and get the chance to relax, as her mother helps out with baby for some of the time.

At this time, having your mother-in-law to stay can be very helpful, but there's a fine line between being helpful and interfering. Also, times change, and your mother-in law's notions of childrearing may be a little outdated, which means you'll have to listen to a lot of unsolicited advice and endure comments about how your routine is wrong, that baby is being fed too often/not often enough, that baby is too hot/cold, etc., along with a whole list of other mistakes and misdemeanours.

There are lots of ways of dealing with a tricky mother-in-law. You could try buttering her up with little presents or sitting down for a one-to-one chat over a cup of tea, or you could just bite your tongue and be incredibly nice to them when they are being unpleasant. But if you have been with your partner for several years, you are probably realistic enough to know that things aren't going to improve after all that time, so just smile, put up with the situation… and wait for them to go home.

If your mother-in-law is planning an extended visit, it's best to arrange the dates so that it begins after your paternity/family leave has ended. Not only does this mean that you reduce the likelihood of potential flashpoints, but also it will be much more helpful to your partner than having lots of people milling around immediately after the birth, then absolutely nobody to help her out after a couple of weeks.

While most men happily accept that having a baby is going to change their lives, there are just a few who can't or won't gladly take up the baton of fatherhood. Even at the announcement of their partner's pregnancy, they declare that they won't let it alter their freewheeling, child-free lifestyle. Well, it's their loss (and their family's, of course), but I would positively encourage every man who is about to become a dad to greet fatherhood with wide-open arms and to accept that his old life is a thing of the past. For many of us it's actually not that difficult. If you've had a good many years as a singleton, then enjoyed life as part of a couple, you'll probably be ready for a break from gallivanting around, and besides, having a child will be the start of a new, fulfilling and exciting chapter in your life.

dealing with a change in lifestyle

Apart from accepting that things will be different, the easiest way of dealing with a change in lifestyle is to reconsider your priorities. Although it's important that you do meet up with your friends occasionally, you need to put your family first. This means that you can't spontaneously accept invitations to go to a pub, club or a soccer match, and if your partner gives you a green card to go out, don't abuse this by then going out every night in succession.

When I first became a dad, friends would still invite me out every evening after work, but I generally turned them down, as I felt a sense of duty to go home, along with a desire to catch up with what had been happening with our son during the day. After a while, the invitations died away and I felt slightly left out. However, most of those folk now have children of their own, so everyone is in the same boat and much of our socializing now includes the kids.

When you go back to work, you might feel jealous of your partner, thinking she's having a blissful time back home looking after baby. This may be true for some, but the reality is that many women will be exhausted after a night up feeding every few hours, coping with their own recovery from the birth or having to calm a fractious baby. So, even if you have put in an eight-hour day at work, you won't be able to return home, put on your slippers and slump in front of the TV. See what needs doing – vacuuming, laundry or preparing supper. Alternatively, get up 20 minutes earlier in the morning to get on top of the chores and, of course, to make your partner a welcome cup of tea.

It's not just keeping up with the domestic chores that will help your partner out. She might not have had five minutes to herself during the day, so give her some space by putting in some quality daddy-baby time while she has a soak in the tub, goes for a jog or takes a well-deserved nap.

helping your partner out

getting stuck in

I remember reading an interview with a celebrity who quite proudly declared that he hadn't been present at the birth of any of his four children and that he had never once changed a nappy. Unbelievable! Although it's entirely his right to choose what to do (and an issue that must have been discussed by him and his wife), I think such an old-fashioned attitude to fatherhood belongs in the Stone Age and is not something I would have expected to hear in the enlightened 21st century.

Surely there is little point in having children if you don't intend to become fully involved with them? Changing nappies, bathing baby, getting him or her dressed or feeding them if they are on formula – all these humdrum tasks give you precious and valuable time with your baby, helping to develop the bond between the two of you, as well as giving your partner some time out if she is feeling exhausted or overwhelmed. Apart from helping your relationship with your child develop, it can also be hugely rewarding and enjoyable, and lead to some amusing incidents that you can use to embarrass them with when they are older… not that you'd want to, of course!

Sometimes it's not machismo that prevents a man from getting involved, but something much more irrational. A friend of mine quite happily took care of his first-born son, but he felt much less confident after the birth of his daughter, as he had absolutely zero experience of little girls and was almost too nervous to pick her up. My advice to him was to get over his fears and to get stuck in. Our children are only babies for such a brief period of time, and you'll never have this precious opportunity for early bonding ever again.

the poo expert…

It's highly unlikely that you've ever had a
desire to closely inspect the contents of a baby's
nappy, but from now on you'll have no choice
and will soon notice that baby's faeces regularly
change their consistency and hue. Although this
may seem quite alarming to beginners, it is in
fact entirely normal. Your baby's poo will vary
depending on age and diet, and it can also act
as a warning sign if there is something wrong.

For a couple of days after birth, your baby's poo will be sticky and greeny black. This is usually nothing to be worried about – it's a sign that his or her body is functioning properly as the meconium, a substance that builds up inside the baby's intestines over the course of the pregnancy, is ejected from the body. However, if your baby has dark green poo at a later stage, and is passing it for longer than 24 hours, then it is best to visit the doctor. The discoloured stools could be caused by too much lactose, or overfeeding or underfeeding, and it may also be due to a stomach bug.

With breast-fed babies, the contents of a nappy might be mustard yellow one day and a yellow with green specks in it the next. The texture is often quite grainy. Bottle-fed babies tend to have poo that is bulkier, due to formula milk, but again the colour can range from pale yellow to brown.

Unlikely as it may seem, you will soon recognize all the different shades and textures of your baby's poo and become as proficient in understanding them as an amateur fortune-teller is at reading the tea leaves. In most cases, a change in appearance is nothing to worry about, but don't hesitate to make an appointment with your doctor if you are worried, and especially if your baby has diarrhoea.

what to do if baby is unwell

Before baby came along, you only really had to look after yourself, and any cold, stomach bug or headache was easily dispatched by either taking to your bed or dosing yourself with medication. However, a baby's lack of communication, your overwhelming desire to protect them and your insufficient knowledge of bringing up children means that you are likely to become jittery every time they so much as sneeze for no apparent reason.

This reaction is perfectly understandable, and many first-time parents will have paid several visits to the doctor because they are worried that their child has an illness that could cause them serious harm. When my kids were babies, we became very well acquainted with the emergency doctor. In the first few months after he was born, my son would sometimes develop a soaring temperature/fever

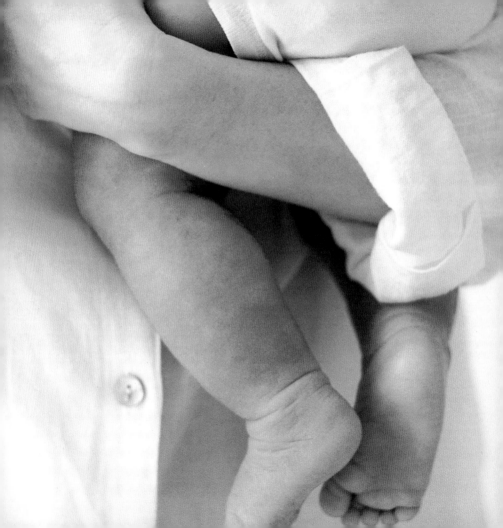

that would not come down, would cry constantly or scream as if in pain, or projectile vomit. For some strange reason, these symptoms always manifested themselves late in the evening and, after we had convinced ourselves that something was seriously wrong, we'd dial the emergency doctor's number or even head to the nearby hospital in a terrible panic. Invariably, of course, it would turn out to be no more than a minor ear or throat infection and we would be given some medication or even told it would simply clear up of its own accord. Of course, I often felt embarrassed to visit the doctor on such a regular basis, but I don't regret it for one minute. Better safe than sorry, and most doctors do understand the anxieties of new parents.

If your baby is unwell, it's worth looking at the illnesses section in a guide to bringing up babies, or consulting a medical dictionary on children's ailments. Choose the most up-to-date volume you can find, with lots of colour photographs to help you identify any signs or symptoms.

your finances

If both you and your partner were working full-time before baby arrived, then you might have been used to enjoying a fairly comfortable standard of living, but when your partner takes maternity leave (or even gives up work altogether), your joint income may be reduced. Of course, this change can have a big impact on your finances, and some families find it hard to cope on a lower income, so make sure you sit down and talk about your finances, working out what all your incomings and outgoings are, while seeing if it's possible to make any cutbacks that would make life easier. Once you have drawn up a budget, then you can plan accordingly and ensure that you don't overspend, making both of your lives a lot more stress free.

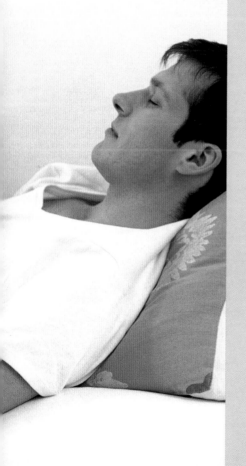

your relationship

It's a fact of life that after she has given birth, the last thing on your partner's mind will be her sex life. Doctors usually say that it's fine to resume sexual relations after six weeks, but many women are not ready after this time, either physically (if they had a problematic birth) or emotionally. Your partner may take

up to six months to recover from the birth, and although you may find yourself becoming frustrated by the lack of intimacy, you have to give her as long as she needs. Rather than sulk about it or resort to emotional blackmail, be a grown-up and try to understand what a life-changing experience she has been through, and that bringing up a baby in the early days can be exhausting. To rekindle the flame, woo her again – bring her flowers, surprise her with little gifts and, when she is ready, arrange for a neighbour, friend or family member to look after the baby one evening so that you can go out for dinner together. Before you know it, your relationship will be back on track.

Another, much rarer issue is that some men can be turned off the thought of sex after witnessing their partner give birth. If she is interested in resuming your sex life but you feel as if the spark has gone after watching her give birth, there's only one solution. You have to get over it. She experienced birth so that you could start a family, so open up about your feelings and you can start moving forward together.

important practicalities

what will you need?

If your home is a temple to minimalism, then you might like to reconsider whether you want to start a family. Of course, I'm only joking, but it is amazing how having a baby requires you to acquire an enormous amount of paraphernalia. Your first visit to a baby superstore will open your eyes to the sheer volume of products that are available. Fortunately, you don't need everything that's being offered, although several items are necessary, such as an infant car seat. And although you probably won't glean much enjoyment from shopping for clothes, having a baby does give you the opportunity to get your hands on some pretty nifty gadgets!

changing your car

The impending arrival of your first baby usually triggers an urge to change your car. Not for something fast and flashy to celebrate becoming a dad, but for a model that is more robust or roomier than the car you are currently driving.

Most of us have never had to consider others when buying a car before – we've either based our decision on what we like the look of or what we can afford. But from now on, the safety and needs of your family are likely to take precedent. You will instinctively want to protect your new little family as best you can, so if you are currently driving a beaten-up old jalopy that has seen better days, you may want to swap it for a modern machine fitted with more safety features.

Equally important is space. The rule of thumb when buying a family car is the bigger the boot/trunk, the better. As soon as your baby arrives, going away for a weekend, or even a day, becomes an ordeal similar to a travelling circus breaking camp before moving on to the next town. You'll need to find room to cram in a buggy/stroller, travel cot/playard, toys, baby monitor, changing mat and numerous other items, along with your own luggage, of course. Even those who have upgraded their car for a roomier model will find that they completely fill it sometimes, and yearning for a boot/trunk the size of a cargo ship's hold is not unusual.

Not sure whether to get a two- or four-door model? Lifting a baby seat in and out of the car can be an effort with a two-door car. Not only is there the likelihood that you'll scratch the paintwork, but it can be awkward to lean in and fix the seat in place. If you are out and about on a regular basis, a four-door car is much more convenient, but if you don't plan to use the car very often, a two-door model would be fine.

kitting out
your car

To ensure that car journeys run smoothly, it pays to spend five minutes equipping your auto for your baby. Suction-pad or roller-blind visors fixed to the side windows are essential to keep the sun off baby's face. In fact, you'll only forget to attach these once, as any baby is unlikely to remain quiet for long with blinding sunshine in its face.

The recommendation for newborns is that they travel in the rear seat of the vehicle in an infant car seat. You might want to buy a back-seat mirror, which fits onto the rear headrest above the seat and allows you to see baby through your rear-view mirror. On long journeys, keep a bag in the car containing baby wipes, nappies/diapers, a change of clothes and a few toys. This will ensure that you don't have to completely unpack the boot/trunk whenever baby needs changing.

The motion of a car usually helps to lull most babies to sleep, but some may need a little extra help. A few CDs of nursery rhymes or children's songs will be well received, helping to calm a crying baby. Endure the music until baby drops off to sleep, and then switch off the CD player to continue your journey in perfect peace…

infant car seats

An infant car seat is an essential item for keeping your newborn child safe in the car, and without one you may even find that your new life as a family will be delayed – many hospitals have a policy of not allowing you to take your offspring home without such a seat, so make sure you buy one with plenty of time to spare.

There are different types of car seat depending on your child's age, weight and height. Babies up to a year should travel in a rear-facing seat, as these are the safest way of transporting an infant. Once your child has outgrown a rear-facing seat, the next stage is an upright, forward-facing seat with a five-point baby harness to hold your child in place. Both rear- and forward-facing seats are either securely fixed to the seat using a three-point rear seat belt or, if you have a new car, the ISOFIX points (fittings at the rear of the back seat that allow a seat to be attached to the chassis of the car).

To ensure that you buy the right seat for your car, it's best to have a retailer fit it. Never buy a second-hand seat. Even if it looks fine, it may have been damaged and have hidden weaknesses.

choosing a buggy/stroller

Walk into a car showroom and you expect to be confronted by a fleet of different models in a bewildering range of hues, shapes and sizes. Making a decision isn't easy and the well-rehearsed patter of the car salesman makes choosing the perfect vehicle even more exhausting.

Fortunately, you won't have to endure the hard sell from a pushy member of staff when you go shopping for a buggy/stroller (unless you're unlucky enough to walk into a store managed by an ex-car salesman who has had a career change), but don't count on being in and out of the shop in five minutes. Many large baby superstores can stock over 50 different models, so deciding which one to choose is going to be a head-scratching experience.

Should you choose a three-wheeler or a four-wheeler? A traditional model or a head-turner that looks as if it's been beamed down from a sci-fi movie? Do you follow your parents' advice and go for something sensible and practical, or do you raid your piggy bank so that you can buy the designer buggy/stroller that all the glamorous celebrity mums can be seen pushing in the pages of glossy women's magazines?

As with buying a car, picking a buggy/stroller is largely down to personal choice. If you're the sort of person who'd rather be seen in a glossy sports car than a reliable estate/station wagon, then you're more likely to go for a fashionable model so that you can revel in the admiring glances as you push it along the street, rather than a utilitarian design that will fail to draw any attention at all.

Whatever you go for, there are some key points to bear in mind before parting with your money. Firstly, measure the boot/trunk of your car. I have known people to go into the shop, fall in love

with a buggy/stroller, order it and have it delivered... only to find it doesn't fit into the boot of their car unless they spend 10 minutes manipulating it into position (generally scraping their hands and the interior of the car to shreds in the process), or they have to take the wheels off first. Life is too short for such a palaver, so get the tape measure out before you hit the shops and avoid creating any problems for yourself.

Remember to ask how long the buggy/stroller will last. Newborn babies need to lie flat, but not all models allow for this, and thus some are not recommended from birth. However, there are plenty available that have a moveable backrest that enable them to be used from birth until baby would prefer to be walking. These are good if you are on a budget, or are looking for a long-lasting buy. A pram/baby carriage created specifically for newborns will have to be upgraded when they are around six months old and want to sit up and watch the world around them.

Some buggies look as if they are straight out of a James Bond movie – fitted out with lots of gadgets, including moveable handlebars, adjustable leg rests and an oil-slick sprayer similar to that of 007's Aston Martin DB5 in *Goldfinger* (actually, I made that last one up). Although some of these features might be useful, the more bits and pieces a buggy/stroller has, the greater chance there is that something will go wrong. If you're the kind of person that breaks things easily, go for a standard model without any of the frills.

Although you might be able to bag a bargain online, always check models out in person before placing an order. This allows you to see how easy the buggy/stroller is to manoeuvre by pushing it around the shop, to check whether you can lift it comfortably and to test whether you can open and close it without having to enroll on a 10-week course in advanced buggy/stroller folding at your local college. Happy motoring! Sorry, I meant buggy/stroller pushing...

kitting out
the nursery

Any idea what the most essential item for any nursery
is? Yes, of course, it's a cot/crib. There are so many
available that choosing one is largely dependent on
cost and whether it will suit the style of the room.
However, it may be worth seeing whether any friends
or family have one that they can pass on to you – both
of my children used the same cot/crib, which was
passed on to me by my parents, who had stored it in

their house for over 20 years, where it was last used by my brother. Now it has been passed on again and is currently occupied by my niece. Why buy new when, with the addition of a new mattress, you can recycle something and keep it in the family?

Another popular piece of furniture is a changing station. With storage space beneath, these allow you to change baby at a comfortable standing height, rather than kneeling on the floor or bent double. A cheaper alternative is to use a simple changing mat on a chest of drawers. Bear in mind that both a changing station or a chest of drawers must be used with extreme caution once your baby can roll.

Unless you're slightly odd, you will not enjoy the smell of dirty nappies, so all hail the nappy wrapper/diaper disposal system. This device looks like a small wastepaper bin, but contains a cassette of scented antibacterial film. To use, simply open the lid, pop in a dirty nappy/diaper and twist a wheel to seal it in the film. A bin can hold up to 28 dirty nappies/diapers before it needs emptying, so you won't

have the chore of popping out to the rubbish bin/trash can every time baby is changed (usually quite a few times a day).

Don't go crazy buying everything that's available for the nursery, because you won't need it. Apart from the items mentioned, the only essentials are a baby monitor and a thermometer. Oh, and a chest of drawers or wardrobe to store all baby's clothes, bedding, towels, nappies/diapers and plethora of lotions, potions and creams...

buying clothes

A new baby's arrival usually results in a flurry of gifts from friends, family, work colleagues and neighbours. Although these might include a memento that your children will be able to keep for life or something for the parents (champagne or a bottle of single malt whisky for me, please), in my experience they tend to be clothes. Not just any clothes, but lot and lots and lots of onesies, sleepsuits and body suits.

Although these are useful, newborn babies grow so quickly that they might never have worn some of them before you have to replenish the supply in bigger sizes, after about three months. Rather than having a glut of these items crammed into drawers, it is better if you can orchestrate it so that you buy the newborn clothing, which you would do anyway as part of your planning, then suggest to any well-wishers that they

might buy clothes that baby can wear after six months or even from 12 months old.

So what do you need? Well, the newborn's wardrobe should contain a selection of bibs, hats, scratch mitts and socks. You will need sleepsuits, bodysuits and all-in-ones/onesies – about seven of each should suffice, but obviously the more you have, the less often you will have to run the washing machine. And don't forget that a few cardigans, a blanket and a coat will be necessary when you take baby outdoors for the first time.

safety issues

Perhaps the most effective way to protect your newborn child is to use your own eyes, intelligence and intuition, but there are a number of hi-tech gadgets available that will provide peace of mind when you are unable to be in the same room as baby.

A baby monitor or alarm is an essential device to keep track of your baby's movement and breathing while the infant is asleep. They generally come as a two-part kit: a baby unit for placing close to the cot/crib, and a parent unit that can travel around with you, whether you are in the kitchen rustling up a meal, pottering in the garden or relaxing in front of the TV. There are many to choose from, with varying degrees of sophistication, different special features and a wide-ranging price scale.

Some monitors offer simple audio monitoring of sound and movement, while others allow you talk to the baby through a speaker, or play recorded lullabies to calm them down if necessary. Some top-of-the-range devices even have built-in cameras (including night-vision cameras) that allow you to check on baby while he or she sleeps. What you choose is a matter of personal preference, but if possible, choose a model with a screen display that allows you to monitor the temperature of the nursery or the room where baby sleeps. It's also a good idea to keep a thermometer in your baby's room, which should be kept between 16 and 20°C/61 and 68°F.

Another gadget you might want to consider is a breathing monitor or apnoea alarm. This is attached to baby's nappy/diaper, and if breathing stops or appears to stop, it will tickle the baby. If this has no effect, an alarm will sound.

When your baby becomes mobile, you will need to completely baby-proof your house with stair gates, socket guards and fireguards, as well as locks for your kitchen appliances, doors and cupboards.

choosing toys

Even if you would like to rush out and buy a slot-car racing track, a football table or a remote-control helicopter, restrain yourself. If you are one of those soon-to-be dads who sees having a baby as a good excuse to relive your own childhood or to buy all the

toys you never had, you are going to have to be patient and wait several more years until your baby is ready to play with all the exciting stuff.

Newborn babies have very simple tastes, basically because they don't really do anything, and they are easily entertained by a few key toys. As they spend a lot of time in their cot/crib, it pays to get a baby mobile – those that play soothing music are great and may even help to get them off to sleep. A play mat, sometimes called a baby gym or jungle gym, will become a key toy. Babies enjoy spending time rolling and kicking on mats made from a patchwork of tactile materials, and those with arches and dangling rattles and squeakers will remain alluring until baby starts to crawl.

Soft books have a mesmerizing effect on babies from about a month old, along with having corners that are great for sucking and chewing, so buy a few whose pages feature high-contrast colours or patterns. You could also encourage a budding talent for music with some wrist or ankle rattles covered in soft material – babies soon learn that they can make sounds by shaking their legs or arms.

Unless you are a dad-to-be and have read this book from cover to cover in one sitting, then the likelihood is that you have now lived through all the early preparations, the birth and the first few months of life as a family, and have made it to the other side. For some this process might have been a breeze, and for others not quite so easy, but you've made it – congratulations! You are no longer a learner new dad, but a fully fledged expert in fatherhood. Well done!

congratulations! you've passed the 'new dad' test

picture credits

Key: a=above, b=below, r=right, l=left, c=centre.

© Stockbyte
Pages 6, 11, 13l, 16, 17, 18, 21, 23r, 29,
33, 43r, 44, 53, 55 inset, 57, 71, 110, 111

courtesy of Mamas & Papas
www.mamasandpapas.com
Pages 2–3, 45, 46, 47, 58, 60–61, 83,
89, 91, 92

Photolibrary.com
Pages 32, 42, 84, 87, 88

courtesy of Stokke Care
www.stokke.com
Page 64

Babyarchive.com
Catherine Benson Page 66l;
Poppy Berry Page 78

Commissioned photography
© Ryland Peters & Small

Peter Cassidy
Page 62

Vanessa Davies
Page 86

Chris Everard
Page 24

Winfried Heinze
Pages 5, 63, 70, 73b, 94–95 Sophie Eadie's
home in London (The New England Shutter
Company www.tnesc.co.uk), 96l & 97 Malin
Iovino Design (iovino@btconnect.com),
104 (www.grosfield-architects.nl)

Daniel Pangbourne
Pages 20, 107l

Kristen Peres
Pages 27, 28, 49, 52

Claire Richardson
Pages 1, 31, 59, 68–69

Debi Treloar
Pages 8, 13r, 14l, 19, 26, 41, 66r, 72,
82, 99, 100, 101

Polly Wreford
Pages 4, 7, 10, 12, 14r, 15, 22, 23l,
25, 30, 34, 35, 36, 38, 40, 43l, 48, 50,
51, 54, 55 background, 56, 65, 67, 73a,
74l, 74r, 75, 76–77, 77, 79l, 79r, 80, 94l,
94c, 96r, 98, 102, 103, 105, 106, 107r,
108–109